Fearless Frontier

Copyright ©2022.

All rights reserved. No part of this publication may be reproduced, distributed or transmitted in any form or by any means, including photocopying, recording, or other electronic or mechanical methods, without the prior written permission of the publisher, except in the case of brief quotations embodied in critical reviews and certain other noncommercial uses permitted by copyright law. For permission requests, write: eggersm@ix.netcom.com

Cover painting, Fearless Frontier, Acrylic by Mary Eggers

Cover Design: Mary Eggers
Editor: Judyth Hill
Book Design: Mary M Meade
Author photo: Tom Roberts

ISBN 978-1-957468-04-4

Fearless Frontier

Poems by
Mary Eggers

This Book is Lovingly Dedicated
to
Lois Read

A dear friend, talented artist,
and gifted poet.

Thank you for introducing me to
San Miguel de Allende,
poet Judyth Hill,
and the love of my life,
Frank Simons.

CONTENTS

I. **For the Love of Words**

Dressed in Rags / 13
Desire Unborn / 14
A Magic Room / 15
Chores / 16
A Writer's House / 17
Ingredients for A Celebration / 18
Insane Search Options aka In Search Of / 19
M & Ms / 20
Mathis Minutes / 21
Ode to San Miguel de Allende / 23
Shadows that Shimmy / 24
Thunder / 25
Giant Steps / 26
Where to Find My Poem / 27
Shimmering / 28
Tuesday Market / 29
Waiting for Words / 30
While Out Walking / 32
Why Be Here / 33
Wondering / 34
An Incredible Slant / 35
A Mysterious Room / 36

Before the News / 38
A Poem of Love / 40
Bald and Beautiful / 42
Fearless Frontier / 43

2. Speaking Out

382 Days / 47
Dry / 48
I Am the Voice / 50
This Fabric / 51
My Story / 52
White / 53
The Grand Illusion / 54
RAGE / 55
Erased / 57
Nine Days / 59
Fall / 60
Headlines / 61

3. Going Deeper

A Gift / 65
A Moment / 66
Choreography / 67
A Day / 68
Found / 69
I Belong Here / 70
A New Road / 71
I Am Now the Hummingbird's Nest / 72
Masks / 73

Slow / 75

Say My Name / 76

A Hole Opens Up / 77

He Sang to Me / 78

Trust / 79

Heart Speak / 81

New Beginning / 82

Words and Pictures / 83

Wanting to Feel Whole Again / 84

His Hand / 85

He Passed / 86

Soul / 87

Acknowledgements / 89

Poppy the Clown aka Mary Eggers

1. For the Love of Words

Dressed in Rags

At the bewitching hour
    when the moon is full,
        there's a midnight junkyard where

music plays from instruments
    that no one touches
        as witches dressed only in color
are twirled around an old scarred
    dance floor by werewolves
        in smooth soft coats found
in empty boxes.

Sitting on the sidelines, some part
    of me craves the freedom to join in
        when a prince dressed in rags
found in a freezer left behind years ago
    for a newer model … extends his hand
        to dance
and gives me a pair
    of discarded dancing shoes …
        that know how to dance.

Desire Unborn

Inspired by Gustav Klimt's
Avenue in the Park of the Castle Kramme 1912

A house at the end
    of a magic forest
holds desire unborn
and soft lines in German
coming from a window on the roof.

Forest trees in an impossible
    dance of joy
        baptize plants
in boundless fields of summer
tended by a chilly gardener
as quiet falls *pure as a peach.*

A Magic Room

A bowl of purple marshmallows
in the room at the top
where copper pennies lay on a table
and blue green iridescent dragonflies
dance the hokey pokey.

This room filled with magic
has opened me to joy … the freedom
    to dream … and new optimism and growth
while weaving my life anew.

Chores

The web tells her they are
"unpleasant yet
    necessary tasks."

For today she will choose
    to say otherwise.

A pleasure hanging laundry
    on the line
a light breeze and sun,
    her companions.

The little market full of color and health,
the orange juice vendor with her
    favorite elixir,
a flower stall.

Her home now more
welcoming because of chores.

Flowers grace the table
    with a few purple additions
from the garden below,
while fruit enlivens
    a handmade bowl
in the kitchen.

The tasks of this day—a pleasure.

A Writer's House

Blue blue—true blue
    a lantern hangs on a yellow wall
its shadow lost in purple and green.

Puddles on stone
    stairs to where …
the rising sun blurs the swirling all.

A snail on a wall
    poetry on a line
a rickety bridge that
    connects me to all.

An artistic line from
    nowhere to nowhere
while joy hovers over all.

Under a canvas of Venetian red
    by the sun by the moon,
        I write about all.

Ingredients for A Celebration

Lots of red, white, blue
    and stars too
orchestra, saxophone, trombone
    Sousa and all that jazz.
Stir in one amazing dancing conductor
along with a very sexy RED dress
a larger-than-life choir of humor and talent…
    Andrews, Keaton, Dion, DeGeneres
    topped with Nicole Parker
    dreaming of flying—on the ground, that is.
Add seven minutes of magnificence
stir in two spicy brothers
    Cuban spices they are.
Sprinkle with Chariots of Fire, Ghostbusters
red, white, blue, true colors shining through
God's blessing and a large wavy ribbon
    of silver fireflies.
All in celebration of America's 240 years.

Insane Search Options
aka In Search Of

Surely they're describing
a much-loved dog
"loyal, attentive, good teeth
own hair, number of puppies
…grown of course."

BORING and an insult
to dogs worldwide.

Plain white bread
no texture, no grit
nothing to hold onto.

The artist's white
of the poet's words…
now there's something!
Full of French Ultra, Alizarin Crimson,
New Gamboge, even
a touch of Opera.

Oh, be still my heart.
Filling me with laughter,
smiles and a spark!

Where do I apply?

M & Ms

Not chocolate, these M&Ms.

One margarita...
perfect!
Yet not one of the Ms
black, white...
as these opposites mingle.

Intense seduction this M,
where hypnotic joy abounds,
a light breeze and
the blue gray of these Ms

create this fusion cuisine from
the music and mountains of
Zandunga.

Mathis Minutes

Johnny sings…
 *"Five hundred
twenty-five thousand
 six hundred minutes."*

Asking—*"how do you
measure a year in a life?"*

How about a day…
one thousand four hundred
 forty minutes
not just any day—the moments of this day.

Of course sleeping, dressing, eating,
 then a long slow meandering
from Refugio to Ignacio Allende
 Elementary School
where the Children's Art Foundation of San Miguel
 teaches creative freedom, fun, and yes, ART.
Cards painted by second graders that bring a huge smile.

Buen Dia Café is next for lemonade with Hannah
 nestled in between yellow and red flowers
surrounded by blue
 head to toe… pure delight!

As I meander home
 stopped by an invitation to adore twelve foot high
poinsettias—gigantic red profusions of color…

then a deep blue sky, lots of stars and a dog barking…
goodnight.

Johnny's reply rings true on this day…
"you measure it with love."

Ode to San Miguel de Allende

Camera clicks
    moments stop.

A bridge built of cobwebs in
a room for a neighborhood
    of the dead,
a family that's gone… no more to be.

Midnight colors cool
    in the dark…
lonely too with shadows that
    wipe out the beauty of all.

Holes in the road
that do not stop.

Bold cloth speaks of
    …a new me.

The road less traveled
    that I want to
travel more.

Visual art that pulled
    me away from
        …the assignment.

A pear I do not know
    replaces an orange that I do.

The San Miguel
    I LOVE to explore
while it explores me.

Shadows that Shimmy

It's how paint flows on paper,
    while light and dark enliven
        a simple straw hat,
how shadows shimmy into imagination,
            turning… flirting
with every possibility—what if…
        we paint an apple turquoise
      or a cat's face magenta
or trees French Ultramarine Blue
    everything leads to the juicy way it all
        plays—within.

Thunder

> *The black sky was a*
> *poem beyond meaning*
> *– Louise Erdrich*

My first evening of jazz
    in nineteen months
needs to be written about, yet how…
    when it is beyond words.
Music thunders though me
    then turns to low tones only
to rise up once more.
    Melting into the music, I'm lost…
in the beat… the bass, the sax
    and Thad's trumpet
all resonating in me long
    after the music ends.
A final high note of my evening
    comes not from music…
there in her full round splendor
    Sister Thunder moon in a black sky.

Giant Steps

John Coltrane

The jazz piece considered most
    feared composition in history
the painting composition the most
    challenging in my history

        circle of fifths
           the color wheel of music
        fifths of *The Beat* two drums,
           two symbols one drummer

Giant Steps and *The Beat*
    full of patterns that fascinate
one with overtones
    the other with undertones

        how demanding these two
           pushing each artist
        to their limit
           especially when improvising

2-5-1 the backbone
    and building blocks of jazz
paint, brush, paper the backbone
    and building blocks of this painting

        Giant Steps and *The Beat*
        art
           and jazz—

        a supreme love.

Where to Find My Poem

I have lots of pens and pencils
that write in every color
this artist would desire
except
they're all out of poems
at the moment.

There are pastels,
watercolors, acrylics and
the brushes, of course,
all capable of writing
my poem
yet... no poem.

There are books of poems
on my shelf all belonging to
... someone else.

OK, so I won't write today
and instead settle in to enjoy
Billy Collins...
and one line—just one
on page 147 tells me where
to find my poem.

Shimmering

He stepped out from
    the shadow
holding stolen lines
       from Scheherazade
    and Dr. Zhivago.

His appearance is
    Lebanese,
when he opened his mouth
      to speak
gold coins pour out
while silver sobs fall from
    his pockets.

It's one in the morning
    I sleep yet
my heart is awake
    and
                open
wrapped in a shimmering scarlet shawl
    as we dance
           until
          dawn.

Tuesday Market

San Miguel de Allende on Tuesdays,
tomorrow… it's a Wednesday market,
somewhere else of course.

What do you need? Bras—got that!
Food—fresh or cooked,
goldfish swimming in a bowl, how about a parakeet, or music—
    yep, that too.

Need a part for your blender, you'll find it there.

My best find you ask…
    …easy…
Tuesday Market's Bass Player!

Waiting for Words

While waiting for words
    the wind picked up
and carried
me off into the deep forest,
      where the faeries
    and leprechauns
are reading Shakespeare.

These are definitely not my words!

While waiting for words
    I fell asleep hoping
I'd find them in a dream… no luck.
I did though find diamonds on a porch
    with a beautiful tapestry
on the wall.
    Duncan was there
to have a serious conversation with me
…don't have time for that,
    I'm waiting for my words.

While waiting… wrapped
    in a turquoise shawl
the warrior Queen came
with a bag of words
    hanging over the saddle of her horse…
a whole bag—none of them mine.

My words would be full
    of laughter, fun,
purple, red, opera would be playing,
    of course!
My words would make everything
    everything
        smile.

While Out Walking

The kisser in total delight
the kissed ready for flight
ignoring me…
while eating.

Kisser slowly comes near
kissee give me its rear
ignoring me…
in favor of food.

Kisser still a seeker
kissee goes deeper
ignoring me…
searching for food.

Kisser adores you
kissee a male
Spicebush Swallowtail
ignores me—as I kiss a butterfly.

Why Be Here

To sit on the porch
    by the shore in ecstasy
lingering while listening
    to waves and watching
lightning welcome the dawn
    a world opened
I imagined a child dressed
    in a garment made
of thunderhead clouds
that someone knitted while
    sitting very still.

Wondering

What's he thinking
    looking so very
deep in thought?

I asked… he said yes
    I said yes,
where is the one I want
    to be sitting here with?

Freddy… father of one
    San Migueler of two years,
done with Mexico city
    too busy, too crazy.
The way I've been feeling about DC…
    am I done as well?

He predicts I'll live here
    what does he know…
that I don't…? Maybe nothing.

He's gone—it was simply nice
    and simply nice was enough!

An Incredible Slant

Mountains, music
           and Mexico
they are all upright straight forward
           incredible.
She stands tall, straight like the mountains
           while her violin's slant
deepens as it engages the mysterious
           and seductive acoustic guitar.
Simmering together - violin and guitar
           come to a full boil
and we are lost in the incomprehensible
           music and improvisation
that slants toward Spanish... of course
           as we sip our margaritas
and yes, this text is slanted, if you don't see that...
           have another margarita.

A Mysterious Room

On a line—laundry
    and marshmallows.
Of course—they go with the Malbec.

I wonder what my guest, Mr. Einstein, is thinking…

A red bird a blue bird
    one slow one fast
both with diamonds in their beak.

What will Mr. Einstein say?

Books on a table
    a touch of purple
next to kiwi and red roses.

Outside a window
    Saturn and the Milky Way
with a hurricane brewing.

What say you Mr. Einstein…

"Why this calls for an experiment—
let's put Saturn's rings
    around the brewing hurricane
add a touch of purple, the kiwi,
    stir in some Milky Way
throw in toasted marshmallows
    bring to a fast boil then simmer slow,

while I toast my success
with a glass of Malbec and pocket the diamonds
...my fee for cleaning out this mysterious room.

You'll find the results of my experiment
    in a book on the table
next to the roses and birds."

Before the News

Three weeks to celebrate 60!
Painting in Italy,
Lucca a walled delight.
Puccini surrounds: there's
Hotel Puccini where I stay
across from the house of Puccini
where he lived
around a corner a church
where an Italian tenor sings
    Puccini.

Morning's spent painting—the trip's purpose.
    Afternoons meandering,
flowers in windows, wine on tables,
art around every corner, laundry on the line,
color and more color, squares, large and majestic,
a carrousel with children's laughter,
evening parades by candlelight,
Italian dinners another delight,
and dessert, Italian gelato oh so… good.

Returning to my hotel to a gesture and smile
he expresses his wishes to join me awhile
Italian cute and half my age
with giggles to bed I go
to dream of Florence to come.

Morning news—front page.
All of Italy mourns a loss.
As we train to Florence,

on this sunny day… raindrops fall from faces,
even the arches of Rialto Bridge are sad,
artists create chalk paintings of his face
on the Duomo plaza.

I heard him sing with friends…
he lives in my memory and
    is gone!

Gone like all of us will be gone,
the hole in Italy's heart will heal,
and his voice will live on,
    after this,
    the day Pavarotti died.

A Poem of Love

She's looked the world over for love
longing for the romantic kind.

There was Germany for work, castles and wine
Switzerland, the Alps and chocolate easy to love.

This city with twilight until midnight
Belgium chocolate and waffles, potions of love.

A whirlwind weekend here, way too short.
Art, markets, the Moulin Rouge, a city of love.

Filling another stop with tulips and windmills
brownies with or without, she's high on love.

Big Ben, BIG stones, evenings of chamber music
balance the days' full of the work she loves.

Islands at 50, dear friend's laughter abounds
Santorini sunsets, selling a car, everlasting love.

In Uganda she fell for people and place
Women's Empowerment Project, so full of love.

Here there were lions, tigers, bears oh my
where all the animals and birds are making love.

Italy for art, Puccini's arias and Lucca
a walled city, the best gelato, what's not to love?

The 1400s, and building of Machu Picchu
stone by stone, hand by hand not a labor of love.

Butter lamps, prayer wheels, Tiger's Nest
A full moon ritual for all the sweetness of love.

Everest with her own eyes, early mornings
circling a stupa, prayers for the world with love.

Mountains, magic and music of Zandunga
her wonder-filled winters of love.

Now at home sitting silent and still
Call it what you may—this, her poem of love.

Bald and Beautiful

You'd say that about
    this couple
every time you saw them.
If you could catch them together
      that is.

I visited here for years
    then… moved in
now it's mine!
Three minutes away
    a place of
          awe and wonder,
if I take my time
    and leave practical at home.
Practical is no friend
    of awe and wonder.

I used to sit at water's edge
    to watch the beaver,
until… they moved in.
Building a big house up high
they're not home often though.

Today there one of them sat
right next to the house
    tall, majestic, beautiful.
One of *my* bald eagles
at the edge of *my* lake…
Bald—and beautiful.

Fearless Frontier

Soft blue with wispy whites
    fading into the stars of tonight.
A glass of wine
    the sound of   children,
flowerpots
    ready to
        welcome color.
All saying yes
    to the fearless frontier
        of this spring.
Tiny bits of green
    open to welcome
the daughters of last year's blooms,
    following in the   footsteps
of thousands
    of years of
Mother Nature
    at her best.

March for Our Lives,
photo by Mary Eggers

2. Speaking Out

382 Days

When they had the chance to ride
they refused to give up
    give in
        or go away.

Sitting between Jerry and Jeff
as tears fall… wondering
how I become an active ally
    for justice for equality.

1955, the story of Montgomery
    were some of Jeff or Jerry's
families there… did they
    walk for 382 days?

Where did their resilience
courage and strength
come from…
    how far have we come?

Will it take a lightning strike
to move us white folks off our…
the time is right now—and yet
    feels far in the distance.

It's midnight, a new day
    perhaps the last… we never know.
Will we   will I
    make a difference today?

Dry

They said 30 years
and it's today.
Nothing.
The last drop
gone.

They said 30 years
it's today
plants
animals, birds,
bees...
gone!
We stole the
last drop!
We let them go first.

Everything gone
before us,
what will remain
for the children
of the children
of the children?

Only billboards
of water hogs
of days past:
my new jeans—2,900 gallons
your leather shoes—2,100 gallons
our new car—39,000 gallons

each microchip—8,000 gallons
times the
56,000,000,000
made in 2015.

We have no water
for the children.

I Am the Voice

I am the voice of the cello and the dove.
I am the voice of Dr. King's words.
I am the voice of my own integrity.
I am the voice of the pain I see in the world.
I am the voice of a deep *gracias*, thank you, *merci* for a life well lived.
I am the voice that stands firm for justice, for refugees, for those without.
I am the purple under belly of the brilliant big puffy cumulus clouds.
I am the oak standing tall for my truth and the truth of others.
I am the voice of the clock that knows time is precious, quickly
running out for our beautiful blue planet,
for polar bear and tiger, for a once wild, free, clear Magdalena river.
I am the voice of Orion hunting for peace.
I am the memories of the Blue Ridge Mountains.
I am the guitar playing softly while holding another in love.

This Fabric

A beautiful fabric this
sometimes shimmering sometimes not
with rich texture

wearing this fabric
it comes alive
with depth and beauty

each fold marking
a passage of time
with darks and lights

it comes only in shades
of brown from
darkest dark to *almost* white

some believe this fabric
is only about color
and chose to not look further

others look deeper and find
what really matters.

My Story

The other poets full of
grace, beauty, courage…
resilience.

A book launch.
My story…
next to normal.
No one trying to scrub
my skin lighter
or iron my hair straighter
parents not needing
to have the
"safety talk."

White

I'm not, what I am is angry
   at being labeled *white*,
this page is white and gets
                no privilege for being so.

   My skin—a very pale
     shade of the brown
  of Burnt Sienna—yet
              my *white* gets all the privilege,
  at the expense of every
brown and black person.

   Caucasian
a term meant to divide us
and it does—even though
              we're all just human beings.

   My heart hurts for
     this injustice,
  black and brown friends,
the pain *white* inflicts on millions,
              my inability to change this.

The Grand Illusion

Running through me
    since before I was
        remaining after I am.

Attaching itself to everything
    in and around me
        stunned by all I missed.

Cracks open this white life
    to a deep sadness
        now I stand very still.

Eyes that begin to see
    my mind searching
        for a path to justice.

RAGE

It's in me…
    and needs to get OUT,
to be released.

RAGE at something we can't see
except for the disease and death left behind.

RAGE at the millions around the world
that starve to death year after year after year.

RAGE at a lunatic president… with a vocabulary of a six year
    old, who cares only about himself and money.
RAGE at those called leaders
    who can't even talk to one another.

RAGE at the illusion that the US is
the biggest and best EVER—at what?… Nothing.

RAGE at the disparity against anyone
    NOT white—what a boring color white.

RAGE at a media that LIES to us
    and doesn't accept their part in where we are.

RAGE at our indifference to the earth…
our home—the ONLY one we have.

RAGE that in 2020 women are still seen,
and acted upon—as sex objects.

NO words will do justice for my RAGE!
My RAGE needs my violence and you

to witness my violence…
    to encourage my release—hear my screams
see my need to TOTALLY destroy something.

Without a release this RAGE will fester
and I.…   will die.

Erased

The women's workspace behind frosted glass
    with a lock where they can uncover.
Here she is *free* to *choose*
    and *chooses* totally covered.

Why? I wondered.

Required to wear an abaya everywhere,
    with what under it?… Don't ask don't tell.
Choosing to wear a hijab when
    in a Mosque.

Still wondering why.

Her image… my lingering question,
    what does totally covered feel like?
A hijab and burqa—become
    my *free choice*.

Air-conditioned hotel to air-conditioned mall,
    a ten minute evening walk in 116 degrees.
With the shopkeeper's help
    I am now covered.

Wandering the mall covered except eyes and hands
    it's now harder to breath, very hot and scary.
My experience… and
    perhaps her's if she uncovered.

The dark walk "home," a lamplight behind
looking down seeing my shadow…
    not me, only a shadow of me…
I've been *erased*.

Nine Days

Or so it should be
    actually it will be
November third
    is of course…
an ordinary day
    on my too ordinary calendar…
Just nine days.

Yet in the year 2020
    it's not an ordinary day
it's a critical day
    perhaps the most critical
will we be red OR blue… or
    blend the two and stand for all…?
Just nine days.

There was a "nine day queen,"
    Lady Jane Grey trying
to maintain religious rule
    that cost her throne and head.
It's said that a soul stays on earth
    for nine days after death…
Just nine days.

The Ninth of Av a day of mourning
    the destruction of the Temples
will this ninth day be the end
    of the soul of our Nation
will we spend it mourning
    or stand for all…?
Just   nine   days.

Fall

Fall
    a season
    an accident
    a nation.

2020
    pandemic
    hurricanes
    floods
    fires
racial divide…
    an election.
What will the children
born in 2020 read
    in history books
  about this year
about us?—The collective us.
Did we stand tall and true
    or…
        did we fall?

Headlines

"EXTRA EXTRA READ
    ALL ABOUT IT
Social Media Murders
    Human Contact."

No longer will there be
    eye to eye soul connections
we will now live without the subtleties
    of body language… laughter,
tears, smiles—all banned.

We will now see others only through
    a lens of words on a page… forever
left out in the cold dark of our own…
        interpretations.

Shalom Mountain Retreat Center, Photo by Mary Eggers

3. Going Deeper

A Gift

A Zebra Swallowtail
walked into my day
 up my arm
        in my hair
and stopped…
    on   my   nose.
I whispered
    I love you,
        I love you,
            I love you.
Searching with its proboscis
showing tiny feet
    staying a minute or an hour.
Touching me
    as I stopped in awe
of a gift given
        a gift cherished.

A Moment

There, just outside my silent window
    you appeared.
Appeared then disappeared
    without my notice.
You've done this for years,
    and this time I saw you for
        a moment.
Present in my silence   that one special
    tender   pink blossom.
You gave me pause…
    beauty… breath
        for a moment.

Choreography

Ginger Rogers light as
    air gliding across
a dance floor.

My mother… impossible
    to imagine her doing
anything as impractical
    as dancing.

Yet she could glide
    through a kitchen
choreographing a delectable
evening meal.

Filling a home with fragrances
of fresh baked bread,
    fried oysters… a n d …
German chocolate cake…
    all in celebration of
my birthday.

A Day

When does it begin - 12:01, first light, open eyes?
How is it counted
    the calendar,
        number of tasks completed or not,
            miles traveled—real or imagined,
                hopes realized or fears dispelled?

Does the day know of any of these or distinguish
    dark from light?
What of my day do I hold in awe and wonder?
How do I measure its preciousness
    moments of silence, awareness of love,
touching or being touched?

Or do I let it slip away unnoticed—lost?
        No!
With fewer before than behind
    days now end as gratitude washes over me
remembering their passing.

Found

Again today I found
    a purple wisteria
it wasn't lost,
    neither was I, yet…
I long
    to be
        found.

Found beyond the
    to do list,
beyond the I am this…
    or that list.

Found in those moments
    when I want to hide
or ones of pure joy.

She turned to him
    standing in that moment
saw him
    the depth, beauty
and soul of him.

If I stand still
    or lay open as the
dogwood blossom,
will I be found?
    Will I allow   myself
to be
    found?

I Belong Here

Where is home?
    auto reply: DC.

Is home a house?
A city?
Places only…to
    hang your hat
    do the dishes and laundry
keeps the rain off.

He asked… "Next week?"
many steps later
"I belong here."

Here in my being
inside of me
    …home

I belong here
It can't burn down
can't be taken away
this inside home
this place where
I open to others
is home.

A New Road

A thunderstorm, divided.
Half goes north
    the other south.

Going east, there's water
    lots of it,
and you don't swim.

Go west "young" woman
where the future is wide open
    except for the mountains
        you'll bump into
and there's no gold to be found there.

Storm's behind you, more water ahead —
    remember you don't swim.

Turn left and go south.
A new road has opened,
one holding uncharted territory
and ways of being
        you don't yet know.

I Am Now the Hummingbird's Nest

My teacher's promise unspoken
a padlock locked my heart
placed it in the sticky center of the spider's nest.

This is not the soft inside of a hummingbird's nest
in a Ficus tree outside a meditation center's door
where she teaches her little one to fly
above the turquois blue match book
that now

lights my fire
opens wide my heart
silences my being
like the sound of white clouds
gently touching my body with joy.

As I release the padlock
and leave memories
of a broken meadow behind.

Masks

Hang in museums,
primitive and native,
like the African monkey mask
used in rituals
when the moon is full.

These are not the masks I want to speak about.

She said…
let the mask speak to you.

To my surprise… it spoke.
Telling of a mostly black and white world
divided down the middle
with a line not to be crossed, yet
the hint of color said
let's take away that line and blend.

He asked…
is it the mask that conceals or reveals?

Poppy, six years old, with a
painted-on facemask

that included a purple tear
revealed love.
The love one gives away to total strangers.
This the sacred mask of a clown
that opens a door that's never closed.

This mask, of cicada wings and bird feathers
said…
let go of—*I don't know how*
in order to
take flight into the unknown.

The final mask
said *Hemlock Overlook*
and when stepping over a decaying log—
take some home and make paint,
and I did.

Slow

It started as slow walking
    which in San Miguel de Allende
is extremely important
    unless, that is, one wants to fall.

Now it seems to have turned from
    a fall, to falling
there are falling leaves, rain, stars…
    yet this falling is different.

This one is scary and delightful
    and not happening slow
we met only two weeks ago
    if I give into falling… will I still stand tall?

Say My Name

"Mary," when heard is like,
the warm sun on chilly days,
rain—gentle on a
      parched land.
You whisper "Mary" and
   a very light breeze
washes over
   my entire body
holding me
   gently in
its sound for a
   very
      long
         time.

A Hole Opens Up

The day before in San Miguel de Allende
    will be sunny just like
        all the others…
only…
    it will be the day before
    a hole opens up
large enough to swallow
        me whole
and empty me of goodbye…
        tears.

I'll pack, write, walk…
do all the things
one does before leaving.

Going where—is home
    there or here?
My heart will be here
    a house will be there.

He will stay… I will go.

He Sang to Me

Standing a long time… no words…
    at *Callejon Blanco* and *Quebrada*
        turning… there, a passionate red painting
            and my reflection… stilled by his singing

standing a long time… no words…
    turning at *Callejon Blanco* and *Quebrada*
        …there, a passionate red painting
            and my reflection… stilled by his singing

there is only
    red
        a touch of blue sky and
            earth tones to ground me.

Quivering
    how can that be…
        my reflection
            appears unmovable?
    Still… silent
        hours… minutes
            with only
                his singing.

Trust

I could feel my left hand tighten
I kept relaxing
no need to tighten
in the hands of someone I
      totally trust

knotted muscle around
my left shoulder blade
I've slept this way since age 10
her screams—imagining his hand
      my body remembers

Dad's anger most nights
Mom in my bed many nights
facing away I learned
to hide my tears and fears
      my body remembers

this knotted muscle tired
from years of holding on
not letting her see my tears
my fear of the screams
      my body remembers

where does this leave me now
all these years later—still and silent
I shared that the time was about trust
"was it something from your past?"
      my body remembers

I quickly brushed over his question
not saying it was… not wanting to share
this is nothing new
yet in this trusting place
       my body remembered.

Heart Speak

My heart said… *let him in*
said, *I won't stop repeating it*
I won't let you rest until you
    let him in.

        It's not that easy… he's dead
        and it's all such a long time ago.

Yes, and it's your work
I'm not letting you slide on this
you've said you listen
when I speak.

        He left when I was five or six
        I didn't understand what happened.

You've been there… you
understand now what happened
help me…I won't heal until you
    let him in.

        His stroke scared me then.
        My stroke scares me now.

I've been murmuring of this
for a long time
now you need to
    …let him in!

New Beginning

Leaving Behind Everything You Know—
    a painting title
        a barren land
            a reset button
                a stroke
…that she said was tiny.

A new beginning…
like no other!
    Without the stuff of life,
that adds so little.

This tender time calls out
    for deeper awareness
        more real silence
seeing rather than just… looking,
    more stillness.

Steps—one by one
into a future filled with
joy…
    love…
        laughter…
            friends…
and a new painting for this
    new beginning.

Words and Pictures

A movie
    and as it turns out
a life… mine.

Juliette the painter,
Clive the writer.
    Chemistry abounds!
Surprisingly, I do both
…yet not always owned both.

Painting yes—mine, all mine, with joy.

Words came with unhappy history.
We have to keep her back a year
    fourth grade twice
She can't read well—glasses—that's the answer.
    It wasn't—there wasn't an answer—not then.

So this two-time fourth grader made up an answer—*stupid*.
    No one knew, so no one corrected her.
She struggled and found ways around
    reading aloud came with terror that underlined *stupid*
wanting to run and hide as they asked
    Are you reading from the same copy we have?

The movie asked, "Which is more important words or pictures?"
As I write this poem, looking forward to reading it aloud
to friends… to share the real answer.
Stupid long ago let go of—thanks to dyslexia.

Words and pictures—both loved—both mine, all mine.

Wanting to Feel Whole Again

Knee surgery
torn tendon
      stroke…
Three's a charm,
    three strikes and you're out,
        or a feminine trinity.
He said "You have been stroked.
    perhaps stroked by God."

Broken…
    instead I feel broken
trying hard to appear
positive, normal…
    and I'm not!

Wanting To Feel Whole Again.

He said "You look great"
with an enthusiasm
    that said
"I didn't know what
    to expect."

I don't know what
    to expect or how
to think or be
    when everything—
the country, my health,
    this isolation
feels broken…

and all I want is to feel whole again.

His Hand

Living alone learning to do…
it *all*,
    no matter what *all* was.
Now lying here on his massage table
    he gently lays his hand on
            the small of my back—and everything…
shifts.

His hand says *be here… this moment…*
is *all*,
    you can let go… not having to do it all.
let go… I've got your back.
    His hand and he are now gone
            replaced with soft music—tears gently…
falling.

He Passed

    In a car, on a train
a float in a parade—no, Mr. Positive
    passed two days ago.

Passed… that sugar-coated word
    trying to soften
the blow that it doesn't
    soften at all.

Mr. Positive is gone
    where?—To the garden.
They both loved the garden
    which once led to Christmas

cards with apples on their heads.
    Maybe he's off to dinner,
Sunflower of course, for vegetarians
    and time with a good friend.

We talked four days before
    about me visiting
and then the news of death came
    Mr. Positive passed.

Soul

Poets write about it, Billy sings of it,
yet what can I say?

When soul is felt
    a stirring within
calling, inviting, beseeching—

       follow.

Follow without question
    without knowing how.
Trust, for you know its truth,
    as it lights the way
one step at a time.

Acknowledgements

Gratitude to someone I know only though his writing—the poet, Rainer Maria Rilke, and his book Letters to a Young Poet, the only book I've read multiple times.

In his letter dated October 29, 1903 he writes, "…one slowly learns to recognize the very few Things… that one can love and something solitary that one can gently take part in." Reading this passage caused me to pick up a paintbrush and become an artist.

And gratitude to Lois Read—we met in 1980 and lost touch for a while, until I visited her in San Miguel de Allende, Mexico. She was still painting then and was also writing poetry. In 2015, I heard her read several of her poems on a retreat and when I arrived home I wrote my first poem—she's encouraged me ever since.

Poetry and art are my "very few Things."

In my poem, "Desire Unborn," the words in italics in the final line are excerpted from the poem "To Go To Lvov" by Adam Zagajewski, translated by Renata Gorczynski.

In my poem, "Mathis Minutes," the lines in italics are excerpted from the lyrics of "Seasons of Love;" 1996; by Jonathan Larson, for the Broadway show, Rent, recorded by DreamWorks.

In my poem, Where to Find My Poem, the inspiring line from Billy Collins is found in Poem on the Three Hundredth Anniversary of the Trinity School in his book Aimless Love.

In my poem, "Shimmering," the lines in italics, "I sleep but my heart is a wake," is from Song of Songs, translated by

Willis Barnes. The lines in italics, "while silver sobs fall from/ his pockets" is in Garcia Lorca's poem (with two different translations of the same poem) The Moon Rises translated by William B. Logan or When the Moon Comes Forth translated by A. Z. Foreman.

My poem, "The Grand Illusion," was "editors pick" and published in 2021 by Colorism Healing in the 2021 Colorism Healing Writing Contest anthology. The anthology features the top poetry and prose submitted to the international Colorism Healing writing contest in 2021.

www.ingramcontent.com/pod-product-compliance
Lightning Source LLC
Chambersburg PA
CBHW071227160426
43196CB00012B/2440